Discard

THE SCIENCE OF

Soil for Compost and Fuel

LINDA
IVANCIC

Cavendish
Square

New York

Library of Congress Cataloging-in-Publication Data

Names: Ivancic, Linda, author.
Title: Soil for compost and fuel / Linda Ivancic.
Other titles: Science of soil.
Description: New York : Cavendish Square Publishing, [2017] | Series: The science of soil | Includes index.
Identifiers: LCCN 2016033401 (print) | LCCN 2016035241 (ebook) | ISBN 9781502621689 (library bound) | ISBN 9781502621962 (E-book)
Subjects: LCSH: Soils.
Classification: LCC S591.3 .I93 2017 (print) | LCC S591.3 (ebook) | DDC 631.4--dc23
LC record available at https://lccn.loc.gov/2016033401

Editorial Director: David McNamara
Editor: Fletcher Doyle
Copy Editor: Rebecca Rohan
Associate Art Director: Amy Greenan
Designer: Stephanie Flecha
Production Coordinator: Karol Szymczuk
Photo Research: J8 Media

The photographs in this book are used by permission and through the courtesy of:
Cover Ben Pipe Photography/Photolibrary/Getty Images, Back cover (and used throughout the book) Sinelev/Shutterstock.com; p. 4 Pavelk/Shutterstock.com; p. 6 Kayo/Shutterstock.com; p. 8 Maisie Paterson/Tetra Images/Getty Images; p. 9 Design Pics Inc/Passage/Getty Images; p. 11 Designua/Shutterstock.com; p. 15 Tui De Roy/Minden Pictures/Getty Images; p. Design Pics Inc./Getty Images; p. 18 NASA/File:TOMS indonesia smog lrg.jpg/Wikimedia Commons; p. 20 Tiia Monto/File:Savelan voimalaitos.jpg/Wikimedia Commons; p. 22 Hugh Threlfall/Photolibrary/Getty Images; p. 23 Moodboard/Brand X Pictures/Getty Images; p. 26 Juliann/Shutterstock.com; p. 28 TinnaPong/Shutterstock.com; p. 30 Julie Alissi/J8 Media; p. 33 Peter Anderson/Dorling Kindersley/Getty Images; p. 34 MBCheatham/E+/Getty Images; p. 36 BMJ/Shutterstock.com; p. 38 Virginia State Parks (https://www.flickr.com/people/37922399@N05)/File:GH Mycenoid mushroom in sphagnum moss (20444052548).jpg/Wikimedia Commons; p. 42 Scott Yee.

Printed in the United States of America

Contents

It can take five hundred to one thousand years for 1 inch (2.54 centimeters) of soil to form.

1 It's About Time

Soil is one of our most important resources. Like air and water, we need soil for life. As a vital part of ecosystems, soil provides a place for plants to be nourished and water to be cleaned, and a resource from which many things are made. Because it is right under our feet, humans have been experimenting with and using soil for millennia. We can even call soil a tool because we have a history of using soil for specific tasks. In many cases, soil has served to meet our practical needs as in growing food, providing building material for shelter, and crafting pottery to carry water. Would you believe that some soils can be used to provide heat and energy?

How does that work? Let's explore the formation of soil; how specific qualities allow us to use soil for a special purpose; and ways we can help to preserve it.

All soil is not the same. There are five main factors that cooperate to form different soils: climate, organisms, relief (topography), parent material, and time. Remember CLORPT for short.

Climate, along with temperature and moisture, impacts how quickly rocks will **weather** and plants and organisms

Climate, organisms, relief, parent material, and time are the five factors that affect soil development.

will decay. In hot, wet climates, soil develops more quickly than in dry or cold ones.

Organisms speed up the breakdown of large particles into smaller particles. The digging action of critters (animals and insects), the growth of plant roots, and bacteria each accelerate soil development.

Relief of the landscape and how much sunlight an area receives will impact how much water the soil will hold. Soils are different along a slope. Soils will be deeper at the bottom of a hill because gravity and water will move particles downhill.

Parent material will affect the type of soil formed. The material can reflect characteristics and mineral makeup of the local bedrock. Or, it may be totally different because it was transported to its location by a river, glacier, or the wind. Parent material is where all soils begin.

Time plays a featured role in the story of soil development. Young soils have not been around a long time and look very different from older, mature soils,

Soils are formed by additions and losses.

which often change over time and become different from the parent material.

When looked at closely, soil is formed by four basic processes. There are **additions** made to soil when water comes in floods or rain; when dust is blown in (adds minerals); and when plants and animal waste **decompose** (adds nutrients).

There are **losses** to soil when water evaporates; when nutrients get taken into plants; when soil particles get

Color tells us about movement and changes that have happened in soil.

washed away; and by the **leaching** (washing away) of nutrients and minerals.

Translocation is movement within the soil. This occurs when gravity pulls water and dissolved material deeper into the soil; when organic matter is carried about by critters and organisms; and when evaporation of water pulls minerals up through the soil with it.

Transformation of the soil happens when one thing changes into something else, like when leaves break down into **humus**; when rock weathers into clay; or when iron minerals in the soil change with oxygen to rust (reddening) or by water dissolving the minerals (graying).

The CLORPT factors and the four processes show us that soil formation is dynamic, meaning it changes all

Don't Look Now ... Destruction!

Destruction is the job of a "decomposer"—something that breaks apart dead things. When any organism dies, fungi and bacteria get to work breaking it down. Mushrooms also join in, as can insects, worms, and other invertebrates. Soil is the link between air, water, rocks and organisms. Soil contains thousands of decomposers that love to live it up and make it yucky with "rot." Decomposition (rot) is vital for finishing up the old and then starting anew.

With rot, the most important things that are released are carbon and other nutrients. Carbon is in all life. When it is released, it can be recycled into new life. Scientists call this the **carbon cycle**. Plants use energy from the sun to combine carbon dioxide from the air with water. **Photosynthesis** creates the sugar the plant needs and uses to grow. Carbon then becomes part of the building

CARBON CYCLE

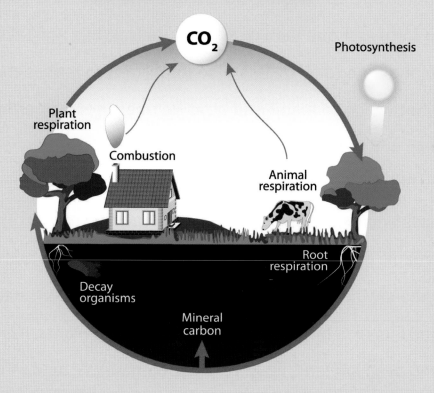

Carbon is moved between the atmosphere, living matter, and the earth through the carbon cycle.

blocks that make up the new plant. And when the plants die, the decomposers show up, and carbon is once again freed into the environment.

the time. It is interesting to discover what kinds of soil are formed in a place.

It is said to take five hundred to one thousand years to form just one inch of soil naturally. While soil takes a long time to form, it is also important to realize that what we do to a soil and how we use a soil can either help or ruin it for future use.

Soil is made up of 45 percent minerals, 25 percent air, 25 percent water, and 5 percent organic matter. The organic matter is anything that once lived, either above or below the ground surface. This is also called **biomass** and includes bits of decaying animals and plants, living and dead bacteria, fungi and **microorganisms**, and other plant substances. This is the material that is used and left behind by the decomposers. Some of the organic matter may be in the form of humus, which is the cellulose, starch, and lignin that come from the leftover structure of dead plants. Cellulose and lignin are the cell materials that give plants their structure.

With its involvement in the lifecycle of various things, soil contains large amounts of stored carbon. And, because plants absorb energy from the sun through the process of photosynthesis, biomass contains carbon and stored energy. When biomass is burned, that stored energy is released as heat. Can soils that contain a large amount of organic matter be used for fuel?

Bogs provide the right conditions for the formation of peat soils.

2 Soil for Energy

Peat is a type of soil that has an organic layer more than 15 inches (38 centimeters) thick. Peat forms when partially decomposed plant material builds up in wetland habitats like bogs. In cool regions, the organic matter is the buildup of mostly sphagnum moss and other acid-loving plants. Besides water, bogs have high acid levels that prevent dead plants from decaying. The partially decomposed moss can also hold a lot of water, and that blocks airflow in the soil. Our decomposer friends, bacteria and fungi, don't work well under these conditions. Peat accumulates where you have plants growing and forming biomass faster than their remains can be decomposed. Peat soil takes thousands of years to develop. The average

boreal peatlands are 4 to 7 feet (1.2 to 2.1 meters) deep. Bogs and peatlands are found mostly in areas where there were once glaciers, such as northern Europe, Russia, Canada, and the United States. There are also some peatlands in the tropics of Indonesia and Malaysia.

Keep the Home Fires Burning

Can you use soil as a fuel? Looking back throughout history, we find that the ancient Greeks and Romans used peat as a fuel source. Some regions in North America used peat for home cooking fires in the 1700s. European immigrants in the 1800s who were familiar with its use in their home countries continued the practice when they came to the United States. Many areas of northern Europe had more peat bogs than trees. It may have been the basic lack of other nearby fuel sources, such as wood and coal, that led to people throwing a piece of peat on the fire to see if it burned! Peat can be used as fuel because it contains a lot of carbon.

Peat is thick and muddy, cut into sod or harvested by milling machines that reduce it to fine granules. Because peat contains 90 percent water, moisture is removed by squeezing, then by drying in the sun or heat. Most of the peat that is produced for energy use is obtained by

Bricks cut from peat are dried in the sun before being burned for fuel.

Natural Disaster: Mega-Fires

Peat fires occur commonly in tropical, temperate, and boreal regions. Peat soils are formed by the natural accumulation of partially decayed biomass. These soils are the largest reserves of organic carbon on earth. Once this biomass ignites, the peat fire smolders, deep within the soil, creeping slowly over extensive areas. These fires can burn for months to years! It is next to impossible

Smoke and haze over a large area of Southeast Asia is from large underground peat fires, as seen in this NASA satellite photo.

to put these fires out. Smoldering fires not only wreck these unique ecosystems, they also add carbon gas to the atmosphere, increasing greenhouse gases.

The leading causes of these fires are drought, drainage of bogs, and changes to land use that result in dry and highly flammable conditions of peatlands. Ignition can be naturally caused by lightning, self-heating, or volcanic eruption; or caused by man through "slash and burn" clearing of land, and arson.

The most studied peat mega-fire took place in Indonesia in 1997 and caused a large-scale air quality disaster. Smoke and haze from the fire stayed in the air and spread for ten months before monsoon rains put out the fires. NASA satellite images show the haze layer expanded over a 1,200,000 square mile area (3,108,000 square kilometers) of Southeast Asia. Poor air quality caused visibility and health problems for millions of people.

milling and generates electricity or heat. Some of the milled peat is made into briquettes (bricks), which are convenient for use as a home fuel. By area, the world's largest peatlands are found in only four countries; Russia, Canada, the United States, and Indonesia. The main countries that harvest and use peat as fuel are Finland, Ireland, and Sweden.

A cogeneration power plant in Finland uses local peat fuel.

Finland has no known sources of coal, crude oil, or natural gas. However, it does have a very large amount of peat, with almost a third of its land area covered by wetlands. Peat fuel is burned for energy in combined heat- and power-generating plants (CHP or cogeneration plant for short). When these plants generate electric power, they collect the wasted heat that is given off and use it to heat buildings and homes. Peat is used in 55 large power plants and 120 district heating plants.

In Ireland, peat is an important source of energy, as the country does not have any fossil fuel reserves. The people of Ireland have been harvesting peat for hundreds of years. Even today, more than 20 percent of homes in Ireland use peat as a source of heat. There is much controversy over peat harvesting today. The use of efficient machines has removed large quantities of peat. Almost 40 percent of Ireland's bogs disappeared between 1995 and 2012.

At Your Service

Another ecosystem service in which soil plays an important role is in natural waste treatment and recycling. Anything that was living and has died will decompose. Decomposition happens naturally by the interactions between microorganisms, soil, plants, air, and water.

Plants are the main source of organic matter. Picture a forest, your yard, or a park, where the trees and shrubs drop their leaves in the fall. Animals also share their waste and the decomposition of

Soil plays a vital role in natural waste treatment and recycling.

Almost 50 percent of waste sent to landfills is organic materials.

their bodies after they die. The broken-down materials are incorporated into the soil by the burrowing, eating, and mixing action of small animals, earthworms, and microorganisms. We should thank nature's recyclers, as we would be knee-deep in garbage without them! Composting is a way to control the decomposition of organic materials into a rich soil-like material that is known as **compost.**

The same process that happens on the forest floor takes place in a compost pile. Both decayed organic matter and compost, when added to a soil, will increase nutrients, build soil structure, and improve the soil's ability to hold water.

No matter where you go on Earth, almost half of all the waste thrown out is organic material. This includes waste from the kitchen, the table, the farm, and the yard. Call them food scraps, leftovers, stalks or grass clippings—almost all of that organic material goes into a landfill.

The purpose of a landfill is to bury the waste in such a way that it will be kept dry, away from groundwater, and not come in contact with air. Under these conditions, waste will not decompose much. A landfill is not like a compost pile, where the purpose is to bury waste in a way that it will decompose quickly.

Organic matter is an essential ingredient in soil. In many ways, the soil is at risk from the farming practices we use and the addition of fertilizers, pollution, and **erosion**. It is important to do things that conserve and safeguard the soil.

One of the smart choices we can make is to collect and compost organic waste instead of sending it to a landfill. Not only do we save space in the landfill, we also create a rich, humus-like compost that can be recycled back into the soil. The ongoing addition of compost provides soil with the texture, structure, and nutrients it needs to support a healthy ecosystem.

The earth is in a constant state of renewal.

3 Gift of the Earth

Soil is like a gift from the earth. Formed when rock is broken up by the forces of ice, water, wind, and heat—with the cooperation of plants from their root action, to the nutrients that microorganisms find after plants die—the whole effort is amazing.

The use of naturally formed soil for fuel and man-made compost is valuable because of its organic matter. In nature, soil takes many years to form. In a backyard compost pile, it is speedier, but it is still the same process that nature uses. It is no coincidence that finished compost looks like soil—dark brown and crumbly—and smells like a forest floor.

What Is Organic Matter?

By now you have a good idea of how organic matter gets into the soil. But there is so much more to appreciate! Like a multipurpose tool, organic matter has many important functions.

Organic matter is the collection of carbon compounds in soil. Organic matter can be divided into two major categories: stabilized organic matter, which is highly decomposed, and the active part that is being used and transformed by living plants, animals, and microbes.

Stable Matter: Count on Me

The stabilized organic matter has been decomposing and transforming for decades and holds tightly onto many

compounds. Not even the microbes can do

Organic matter is vital to healthy soil.

much more work on this material. Almost one half of the organic matter in a soil is considered stabilized. Some of these held compounds work with clay, and actually act like glue to hold together tiny bunches of soil particles. Crumbly soil gives good structure for plants to grow.

This soil glue provides more than just a bond. This organic material also holds on to nutrients and lets them go when plants need them. Like a vitamin we take to release nutrients to our bodies, this matter is also supercharged with nutrients. Healthy soil grows healthy plants.

This stabilized organic matter has one more trick up its sleeve. It acts like a sponge and absorbs water. In hot or dry conditions, the water held in these soil sponges can give plants and the decomposers that live in the soil the water they need to survive.

Active Matter: Got a Job to Do

The remaining organic matter in the soil is either living organisms and fresh material, or is the partially

Making a mini-composter in a cup.

Compost in a Cup

Here's an experiment on composting. You will build two compost environments and identify factors that affect how well each one works. When the experiment is done, review these questions: Can you identify anything in the compost? Which items decomposed the most? Why?

Is there a difference in the quality or the amount of the compost that came from the cup with holes versus the cup with no holes? Why? What factors could have contributed to the differences?

What You Need

Two 16 oz. (473 milliliter) plastic cups, one with

  about five holes punched in bottom and sides,

  one with no holes.

Large bowl

Enough compostable items—vegetable scraps,

  peels, grass clippings, coffee grounds, leaves,

  etc., to fill one of the cups

½ cup (120 mL) dirt or compost

2 tsp. (10 mL) water

Large spoon or small spade

Two pieces of plastic wrap

Two rubber bands

What You Do

- With help from an adult, chop the collected
  organic material into small pieces. Place the
  chopped organic matter in the large bowl.

- Add ½ cup dirt or compost.

- Add 1 teaspoon of water. Mix. If the organic matter is dry, add 1 teaspoon of water.

- Number the cups with a marker. Place two scoops of organic mixture into each cup.

- Wrap plastic wrap on top of each cup and secure it tightly with a rubber band.

- Place the cups in a spot where they will get part sun and part shade during the day.

- Record the date the compost cup was created and the to-be-opened date, five weeks away.

- Once a week, add 1 teaspoon of water, reseal the cup and shake it gently.

- On the open date, spread several layers of newspapers in two piles and dump the contents of each cup on its own pile. Examine the items. Answer the questions posed at the beginning of this section.

decomposing material. Up to half of the organic matter in the soil is the active job site where the decomposers do their work. Here is where soil organisms change organic compounds from one form to another. They eat what is left after a plant dies along with other organic matter, and then create by-products, wastes, and cell tissue. Their work makes nutrients. Regular additions of more organic materials to the work site keep the workers happily humming along.

Soil organisms take on extra jobs when needed. This can include destroying pollutants, controlling disease, and bringing soil particles together into larger

A tablespoon of soil contains six billion microorganisms!

Organic rich soils are the result of great teamwork by micro-organisms, water, oxygen, heat, and plant and organic remains.

clumps called aggregates. When a soil is working, everyone (including the microbes, plants, and growers) is happy.

Recipe for Peat

Peat soils in bogs are unique in that they are formed by layers of partially rotted plants that have built up over thousands of years. There are some conditions that make the organic material stay this way. Peat is wet. Peat is 90 percent water and 10 percent solid matter. Water comes only from rainfall (not from mineral-containing groundwater) and is very low in nutrients. Sphagnum moss is the plant species that likes these conditions. As it grows, the moss makes bog water more acidic.

When the moss plants die, the organic matter is preserved, more or less intact. This is because the moss is acidic, so bacteria and fungi work slowly. The dead peat moss and other plants are crushed by the weight of the living plants growing above them. This flattened matter eventually builds up and forms the peat.

The high amount of organic matter in peat soil is the result of the constant addition of new moss that grows and then dies, and the fact that very little of the moss organic matter decomposes.

Recipe for Compost

Composting is the process people use to convert organic materials into a rich soil amendment. It happens anywhere there is enough organic matter, moisture, and air to encourage the bacteria, fungi, and other organisms that decompose organic matter. Experts estimate that a tablespoon of soil contains six billion microorganisms!

When we compost instead of throwing organic matter in the trash, we save valuable nutrients from being lost forever in a landfill.

The four essential ingredients of compost are: browns, greens, air, and water. Browns are dry and woody plant trimmings, such as wood chips, dried leaves, and straw. Browns are rich in carbon. Greens are moist vegetable and fruit scraps, green leaves, and fresh manure. Greens

are rich in nitrogen. In a compost pile, you want approximately half brown materials and half green materials by volume.

Backyard composting bins produce nutrient-rich compost.

Please note that no meat or dairy items should be included because they can potentially add harmful bacteria that will not only stink, but will also have the potential to make people sick.

Decomposer organisms need air and water to break down organic matter. Turning/mixing and watering the pile provides it with the air and moisture that is needed for microrganisms. The pile should only be as moist as a wrung-out sponge. These four ingredients create the perfect setting for the decomposers: fungi, bacteria, and insects. It can take anything from a few months to a year or more for waste to break down and turn into compost.

Flowering sphagnum moss decays slowly to form peat bogs. Bogs keep organic material from decaying so scientists are experimenting with using peat water to keep food fresh.

4 New Uses for Soil

Humans have been using soil for a long time. One would think that we have investigated all the ways in which it can be used for fuel. Or, how best to make and save organic material from being lost. Well, that is what is so inspiring about us humans. If there is a question or problem to solve, we try to find an answer.

Today, with the advancement of technology, the use of energy has increased in all aspects of our lives. We not only have efficient machinery to harvest peat, we have the knowledge to design and operate power plants that use many other fuel sources. Today, the use of peat for fuel is limited to only those places where other fuel is not available and climate and bog conditions exist.

Peat takes thousands of years to form, and the supply of peat is limited. Peat removal is only one land-use option for peatlands and often competes with other land-use possibilities such as agriculture or preservation.

The latest technology using peat really isn't that new. In order to preserve foods without expensive refrigeration, scientists are looking into using peat water! The Vikings and Scandinavian fishermen traditionally buried their catches in bogs to preserve them for later use. Today, we see that a complex sugar in the sphagnum moss slows the attack of bacteria that causes food to decay.

Peat is mostly used in horticulture, which is the science of growing plants, fruits, vegetables, and flowers. It is mixed with mineral soil and used for growing plants in nurseries. Peat moss is also useful in gardening. Because of its high acidity, peat is added to garden soil to provide the acid environment that certain plants need to grow. And, if added to soil made of sand and clay, it will help the soil hold water.

Compost

Today, there are many types of composting that take advantage of microorganisms decomposing a waste into something usable. Sometimes called organics recycling, composting happens on a small scale in backyards, but also in cities where an entire community collects biodegradables for large-scale community-wide composting. The Environmental Protection Agency (EPA) says that food waste is the largest volume of waste going into landfills. Many areas have services that pick up food waste from restaurants, schools, and hospitals in order to keep it out of landfills.

Large food-producing companies, such as hog farms, have realized that much organic waste is generated when they make their products. Anaerobic digestion uses microorganisms to break down organic materials—such as food waste or manure—without using oxygen. The process produces a biogas that can be used as a fuel source to make electricity.

A soil battery gives energy to people far from other sources.

Using soil for fuel is just another way to say it provides energy. Microbes in soil actually emit electrons as they break down organic material. A student developed a soil battery to help provide power to communities that do not have electricity. This creates power to charge cell phones and also to provide light. The use of LED (light emitting diode) lighting requires only one one-thousandth of the electricity needed to power a standard light bulb.

The role of soil is essential for life on earth. Soil conservation is a combination of practices used to protect the soil. First and foremost, soil conservation involves treating the soil as a living ecosystem, and recognizing that all the organisms that make the soil their home, play important roles in producing a fertile, healthy environment.

Glossary

additions Things that get added to soil; water, organic matter from plants and animal, minerals, energy from the sun.

biomass The living (bacteria, fungi, worms, etc.) and non-living (dead leaves, animals) components of soil.

bog Wet spongy ground consisting of decomposing vegetation, which ultimately forms peat.

boreal Relating to, or located in northern regions with cold climates.

carbon cycle The natural processes through which elemental carbon is recycled in the environment.

compost The decayed mix of plants used to improve the soil.

decompose The way a material is broken down into its basic parts.

erosion The separation and breakdown into smaller pieces by wind, water, and other natural agents.

humus The organic component of soil; typically decomposed plants and animals.

leaching The removal of nutrients from soil or similar material by the action of saturating with a liquid, especially rainwater.

losses Things that are removed from soil by natural events such as erosion, plant uptake, or water evaporation.

microorganisms The bacteria, fungi, archaea, nematodes, and protozoa living in soil.

photosynthesis The process by which green plants and some other organisms use sunlight to create foods from carbon dioxide and water; it generally involves the green pigment chlorophyll.

translocation The movement of materials within the soil by water and biological activity.

weather The physical breakdown and chemical decomposition of earth materials at or near the earth's surface.

Further Information

Books

Lindbo, David L., and others. *SOIL! Get the Inside Scoop*. Madison, WI: American Society of Agronomy, 2008.

Siddals, Mary McKenna. *Compost Stew: An A to Z Recipe for the Earth*. Decorah, IA: Random House Children's Books, 2014.

Silverstein, Alvin, and Virginia Silverstein. *Life in a Bucket of Soil.*

Mineola, NY: Dover Children's Science Books, 2000.

Websites

The Kid Should See This

http://thekidshouldseethis.com/post/75812176267

This video, titled "Inside the Compost Cycle: Turning waste to nutrient-rich soil," explains the value of compost.

The National Association of Conservation Districts

http://www.nacdnet.org/education/soils

This organization provides links to educational materials, including this page on soils.

Science Buddies

http://www.sciencebuddies.org/

Science Buddies provides free project ideas and help in all areas of science from physics to food science and microbiology.

Index

About the Author

As a child, **Linda M. Ivancic** mixed many a compost pile and fabricated Barbie doll furniture from Lake Ontario clay. Today, she rejoices in the awesomeness of the carbon cycle at work and still keeps her finger nails short to play in the soil of her garden. She has written several science books for middle school students for Cavendish Square Publishing.